Everyone Pays Taxes

Antonio Sacre, M.A.

Reader Consultants

Cheryl Norman Lane, M.A.Ed.
Classroom Teacher
Chino Valley Unified School District

Jennifer M. Lopez, M.S.Ed., NBCT
Teacher Specialist—History/Social Studies
Norfolk Public Schools

iCivics Consultants

Emma Humphries, Ph.D.
Chief Education Officer

Taylor Davis, M.T.
Director of Curriculum and Content

Natacha Scott, MAT
Director of Educator Engagement

Publishing Credits

Rachelle Cracchiolo, M.S.Ed., *Publisher*
Emily R. Smith, M.A.Ed., *VP of Content Development*
Véronique Bos, *Creative Director*
Dona Herweck Rice, *Senior Content Manager*
Dani Neiley, *Associate Content Specialist*
Fabiola Sepulveda, *Series Designer*

Image Credits: pp.6–9 Fabiola Sepulveda; p.21 Bastiaan Slabbers/iStock; pp.22–23 Library of Congress [LC-DIG-pga-08593]; p.27 Everett Historical/Shutterstock; pp.28–29 Dragos Asaftei/Shutterstock; all other images from iStock and/or Shutterstock

Library of Congress Cataloging-in-Publication Data

Names: Sacre, Antonio, 1968- author.
Title: Everyone pays taxes / Antonio Sacre.
Description: Huntington Beach, CA : Teacher Created Materials, 2021. |
   Series: iCivics | Includes index. | Audience: Grades 2-3 | Summary:
   "Taxes are the money government collects from people to pay for things
   everybody uses. Taxes pay for roads, hospitals, schools, and libraries.
   Who pays taxes? Everyone pays taxes!"-- Provided by publisher.
Identifiers: LCCN 2020016193 (print) | LCCN 2020016194 (ebook) | ISBN
   9781087605166 (paperback) | ISBN 9781087619408 (ebook)
Subjects: LCSH: Taxation--United States--Juvenile literature. | Finance,
   Public--United States--Juvenile literature.
Classification: LCC HJ2381 .S26 2021 (print) | LCC HJ2381 (ebook) | DDC
   336.200973--dc23
LC record available at https://lccn.loc.gov/2020016193
LC ebook record available at https://lccn.loc.gov/2020016194

5482 Argosy Avenue
Huntington Beach, CA 92649-1039
www.tcmpub.com

ISBN 978-1-0876-0516-6

Table of Contents

Who Pays?

A student wakes up, turns on her light, and eats. She brushes her teeth. She takes a bus to school and back home again. After school, she plays soccer at a local park. Then, she eats a tasty meal with her family.

Who pays for the electricity and water she uses in her house? Who pays for the bus and the school? Who pays for the field where she plays soccer? Who makes sure her food is safe and healthy?

You might say her parents pay for the food, electricity, and water. Her city pays for the bus. The school district pays for the school. The county pays for the field.

These things often cost more than individual people or groups pay. Many of these things are paid for by **taxes**. But what exactly are taxes?

Jump into Fiction

The Super Duper Slooper Book of Slime

As soon as the bell rings, Paula sprints out of her classroom, past the lunchroom, and toward the library.

"Walk!" shouts Ms. Flowers.

"I *am* walking!"

"No, you're not!"

Paula slows to a speed walk and says, "I have to get to the book fair! The new *Super Duper Slooper Book of Slime* just came out. It has a hundred slime recipes, including one for magnetic slime!"

"If I see any magnetic slime in my classroom, there will be no recess for the rest of the school year!"

Paula smiles. "You say 'no recess' about everything, Ms. Flowers!"

"I mean it this time!" Ms. Flowers adds with a grin.

"Okay, fine. Can I saunter to the book fair?" Paula asks.

"Using the new vocabulary—well done! Yes, you may saunter," Ms. Flowers says, laughing.

Paula walks into the library. She sees books stacked on shelves. Excited children buzz around the room.

Paula finds the arts and crafts section. She steps around the little kids pulling out books from the bottom shelf. Paula grabs a huge book with a glossy cover. She looks at the price on the back— $19.99. She takes a bill out of her pocket and unfolds it. "Perfect! And I'll have one penny left over!" she says to herself.

Paula walks to the cashier and hands him the book.

"That'll be $21.49, please," the cashier says.

Paula looks at him, confused. "But it says $19.99 on the back!" she says.

"The sales tax makes it more," the cashier replies.

"But I'm just a kid!" she begs.

"Sorry, kid. Everyone has to pay taxes."

School Book Fair

Super Duper Slooper Book of Slime	$19.99
Sales Tax	$1.50
TOTAL	**$21.49**

Back to Nonfiction

What Are Taxes?

When someone flips a light switch in their home, there is a **system** in place that allows the light to turn on. Companies make electricity. Wires bring it into the home. Workers check the wires and repair them when damaged.

When someone turns on the water, another system allows this to happen. Water flows into a **treatment plant**. It is cleaned and sent back through pipes. The pipes travel to the home. So, when a faucet is turned, the water is there.

It costs millions of dollars to build these systems. One person could not afford to pay for them. People rely on the government to make many of these things happen. The government builds and takes care of these systems.

Miles of Wires

Electricity gets made in lots of places. It is sent to homes and businesses. This system of delivery is known as the electrical grid. The U.S. electrical grid is called the "largest machine in the world." One reason for this nickname is because of the grid's millions of miles of wires!

These power lines are part of the U.S. electrical grid.

Types of Taxes

The U.S. government provides lots of **goods** and **services** for its people. The government pays workers to deliver mail. It pays soldiers to defend the country. It makes laws to protect the people. It helps farmers grow food. The government makes sure products are safe to use. It provides money to build hospitals to keep people healthy.

How can the government afford all this? The government pays for these things with tax money. Taxes are money that people pay to the government. People pay taxes in a few different ways. Two of the main forms of taxes are income tax and sales tax.

Here's an example: If a bus driver makes $800 a week driving a bus, how much money will she take home after one week? You might say $800. But the government takes some of her money first. This is called income tax.

Military Spending

Tax money pays to keep people safe. In 2018, the government spent $54 billion on the armed forces. That's $165 for each person in the country.

Income tax is taken out of the money people earn, which is called *income*. The bus driver makes $800 each week. But her **take-home pay** is less. She likely pays about $80 in income tax each week.

Imagine that the bus driver gives her son $20 to buy a toy. If the price on the toy is $19.99, how much money will her son need to buy it? He will need the price of the toy plus sales tax. He might have to pay almost $22 total for the toy.

For this family, the government collected $80 in income tax and nearly $2 in sales tax. That might not seem like enough money to pay for all the things the government provides. But lots of people pay taxes on things they buy. These amounts add up. The U.S. government collects trillions of dollars each year from taxes. In most years, it spends every single cent.

It Balances Out

Five states do not charge sales tax. Those states are Alaska, Oregon, Montana, Delaware, and New Hampshire. There is a catch, though. These states tend to collect more for other types of taxes, such as income taxes.

Dave's Toy Store

Receipt #0512
March 8, 2021
500 Eastern Drive
San Diego, CA 92101

****

Remote Control Car $19.99

Sales Tax $1.59

****

TOTAL $21.58

There are a lot of different types of taxes. Most tax types fall into three groups: income, goods and services, and **property**. A lot of people pay taxes in all three groups, but some people do not. For instance, some people do not earn incomes. They might be too young to work. Or, they might spend their time taking care of others. They don't have to pay income taxes because they don't have incomes. But these same people probably pay sales taxes on the goods and services they buy. Or, they may own their home, so they pay property taxes.

Homeowners pay property taxes.

Most companies pay taxes too. Companies that sell food, cars, or other goods and services pay taxes on the money they make. Some companies don't pay taxes. Those companies are **nonprofits**. They serve people and communities. The government does not tax these groups.

You Can Help!

There are more than a million nonprofits in the United States. These groups help people find food, housing, clothing, and more. People give their money and sometimes their time to help these groups.

Tax Dollars at Work

Taxes pay for things people see all around them. Tax money pays for police officers and firefighters. It pays for public school teachers and roads. Tax money pays for public parks. Some inventions used every day were paid for by taxes. The internet and a lot of lifesaving medicines might not exist without taxes.

Taxes also pay for things that can't be seen. Taxes give people clean water. They give people **reliable** energy and safe food. Taxes pay to help people who are too old to work. They help sick and hurt people. Tax money pays for elections. It pays people to make and enforce laws. Tax money can even be used to make sure people pay their taxes!

What Does It Cost?

Communities in the United States spend about $113 billion a year on water. That comes out to about $345 per person. The money helps to supply water and treat sewage.

So You Don't Like That Tax?

The United States has a **democratic** form of government. That means that everyone has a say in how it is governed. People speak their minds in many ways. They vote. They email and call their leaders. People write letters to newspapers and post online. They talk to their neighbors. They join **councils**. Most schools have councils. Many neighborhoods do too. People often speak about their concerns at council meetings.

neighborhood council meeting

Think and Talk

How does the photo support the main idea of the paragraph?

Some people might not like how their tax money is being spent. Or, they may think that taxes are too high. They can speak out about these issues. If they don't agree with what the government is doing, they can vote for new leaders. If people think new taxes are needed to solve a problem, there are ways to share those ideas too.

These students want tax money to go to schools.

The United States was formed because people wanted to have a say in their government. To be exact, they were upset about taxes! The king of England taxed people living in the **colonies**. They had to pay, but they did not get a say in the government. They could not choose how the money would be spent. People got mad and fought to have their rights. It took years of fighting, but they won.

"No Taxation without Representation"

In 1773, colonists dressed as American Indians dumped tea into the Boston Harbor. They were mad at King George III. He had made a new tea tax. Colonists were tired of paying taxes without having a voice in government.

At first, almost no taxes were collected in the United States. Then, some special taxes were charged. For example, the government charged taxes to help pay for wars. When the wars ended, so did the taxes.

The country grew and soon needed more money. It needed to build railroads and schools. It needed hospitals and armed forces. People knew that the nation needed these things. They agreed that all people should help pay for them.

How Taxes Are Collected

As the country grew, so did its needs. The government found different ways to tax people. Today, when people buy gasoline, they pay a tax. When people are given a lot of money, they are taxed. Workers pay a tax on what they earn. The company that hires them pays taxes on what they earn too. When people win the lottery, a lot of it goes to taxes!

It is difficult to figure out what is fair when it comes to taxes. Because of this, tax laws change nearly every year.

Americans pay an average of 50¢ in taxes per gallon of gasoline.

Companies pay about one-tenth of an employee's earnings in taxes.

Lottery winners pay at least one-fourth of their winnings in taxes.

Changing Rates

Sometimes, the government collects too much in taxes and pays it back. This is called a *tax refund*. Other times, the government spends too much money. The next year, they will have to raise taxes.

The part of the government that is in charge of collecting taxes is called the Internal Revenue Service, or the IRS. People and companies pay taxes to the IRS throughout the year. By early April each year, people have to figure out if they owe more money to the IRS. It's all a big math problem. Some people figure out their taxes on their own. Others pay tax people to help them figure out what they owe.

Some people have to pay more money to the IRS. Some may owe nothing, while others even get money back. That happens when they have paid too much throughout the year. The government tries to find a fair balance. It does not want to collect too much. But it needs to pay for the goods and services it provides.

The IRS

President Abraham Lincoln (center) started the IRS. One reason it was formed was to help pay for the Civil War. About 80,000 people now work for the IRS.

Everyone Pays

A person works hard at their job. It might not seem fair that some of the money they earn is taken away from them in taxes. Then, someone buys something with the dollars they earn. It might not seem fair that they also have to pay taxes on the thing they buy. But tax money helps everyone.

Taxes are used for things we all need. Sometimes, tax money is used to invent things we didn't even know we needed! People are happy when taxes are well spent. Other times, people think that tax money is wasted on things they don't need. People can make their voices heard about the way their tax dollars are spent.

Think and Talk

How is this library similar to your school or local library? How is it different?

Taxes pay to operate this library.

Glossary

colonies—distant territories that are under the control of other nations

councils—groups that are in charge of managing things

democratic—related to a form of government in which people vote for their leaders

goods—things that are made and can be sold

nonprofits—groups that do not exist for the purpose of making money

property—something, such as land, that is owned

reliable—dependable; able to be trusted

services—work done by groups that does not involve producing goods

system—an orderly plan or system for completing a function

take-home pay—the money that people earn after paying taxes and other fees

taxes—money that people and businesses pay to support the government

treatment plant—a place where waste is cleaned so that it is not harmful to the environment

Index

Civics in Action

Everyone pays taxes—even kids! Some people don't mind paying taxes. They know they are helping the nation. Other people feel they pay too much in taxes. They would rather keep their money. How do adults you know feel about paying taxes? Conduct an interview to find out.

1. Choose a person at home to interview.

2. Write their name, and explain how they are related to you.

3. Ask them what they like about taxes.

4. Ask them what they do not like about taxes.

5. Write their answers and compare them to the answers a classmate receives.

Read and Respond

1. What do taxes pay for?

2. If you wanted to change a tax law, how could you change it?

3. How do the photographs on pages 24 and 25 support the text?

4. Do you think it's fair that people have to pay taxes on items they buy? Explain.

Everyone Pays Taxes

Taxes are money the government
collects from people to pay for
things everybody uses. Taxes
pay for roads, hospitals, schools,
and libraries. Who pays taxes?
Everyone pays taxes!

121674

ISBN-13: 978-1-0876-0516-6

90000

9 781087 605166

TCM | Teacher
Created
Materials

Lexile®: 640L

iCivics

Media Matters

Heather E. Schwartz

TCM Teacher Created Materials